We start with a large point in the middle which we then outline with small points.

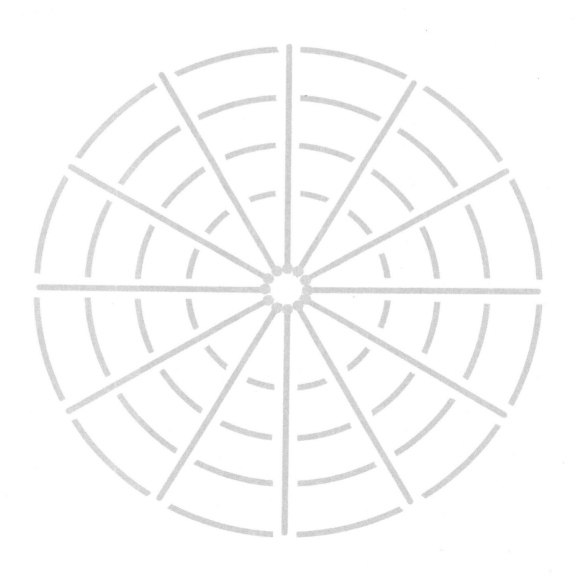

Paint the next points staggered and always get a little bigger, starting with the lightest color.

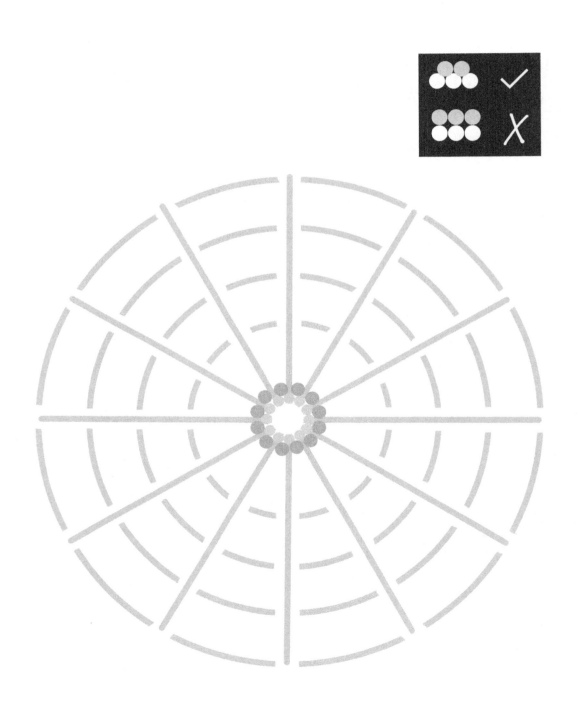

Fill the whole area with dots and get darker and darker with the color.

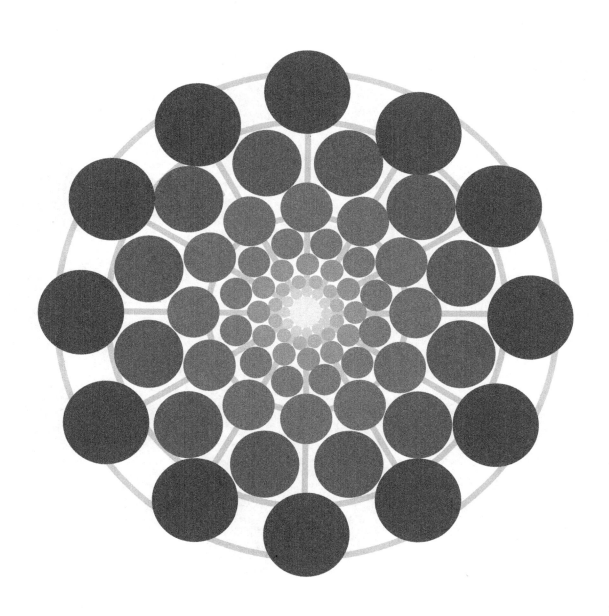

Small dots in the spaces.

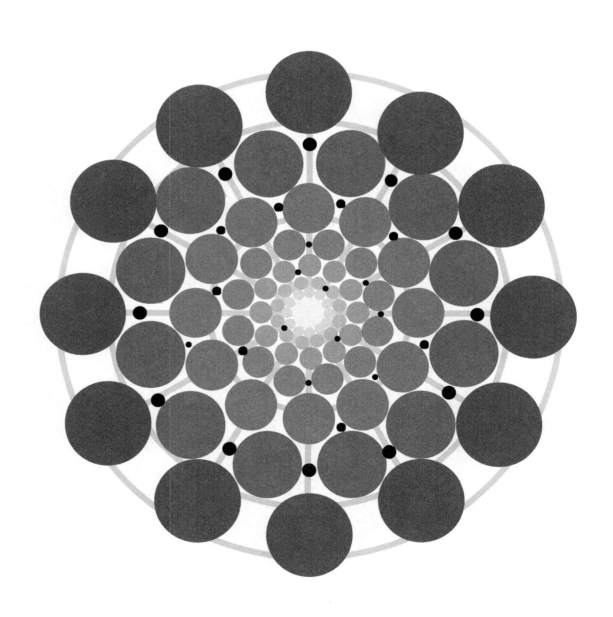

Points to points with the color of the previous row.

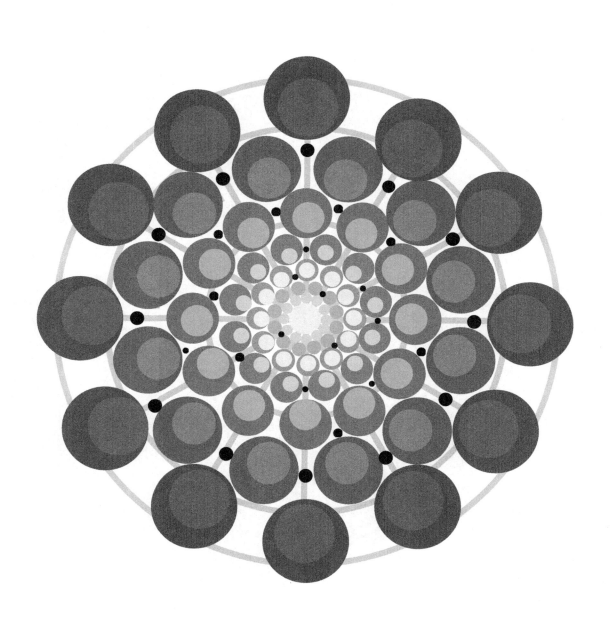

A few more points for decoration and your dot mandala is ready. :)

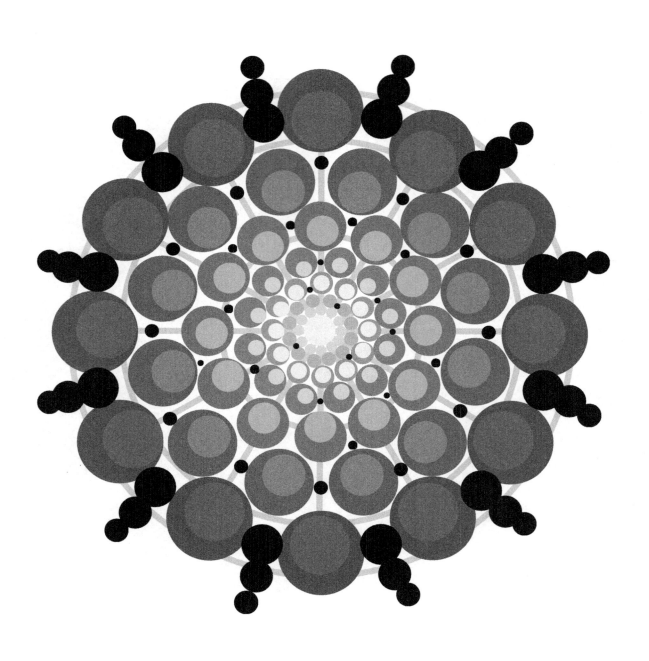

Now it's your turn. Design your dot mandala according to your ideas.

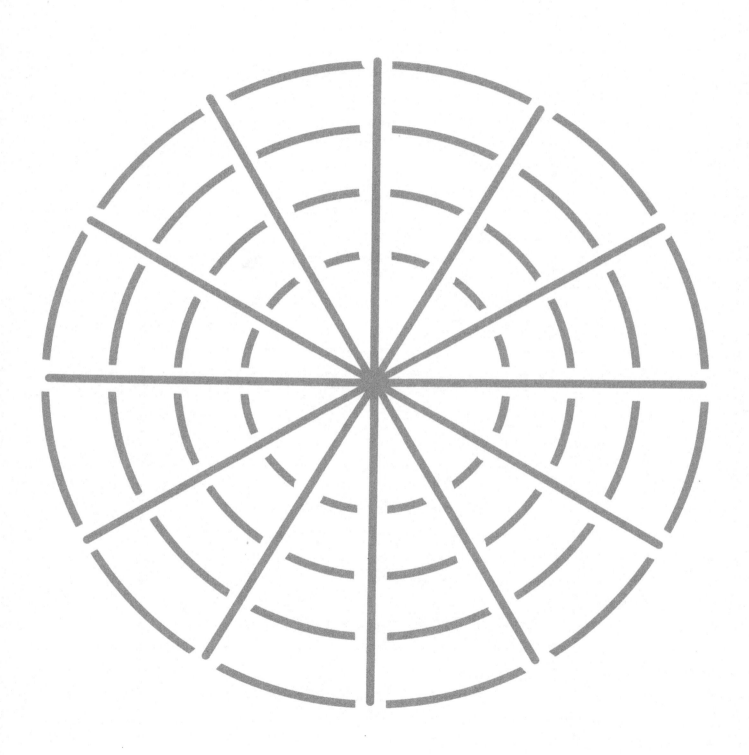

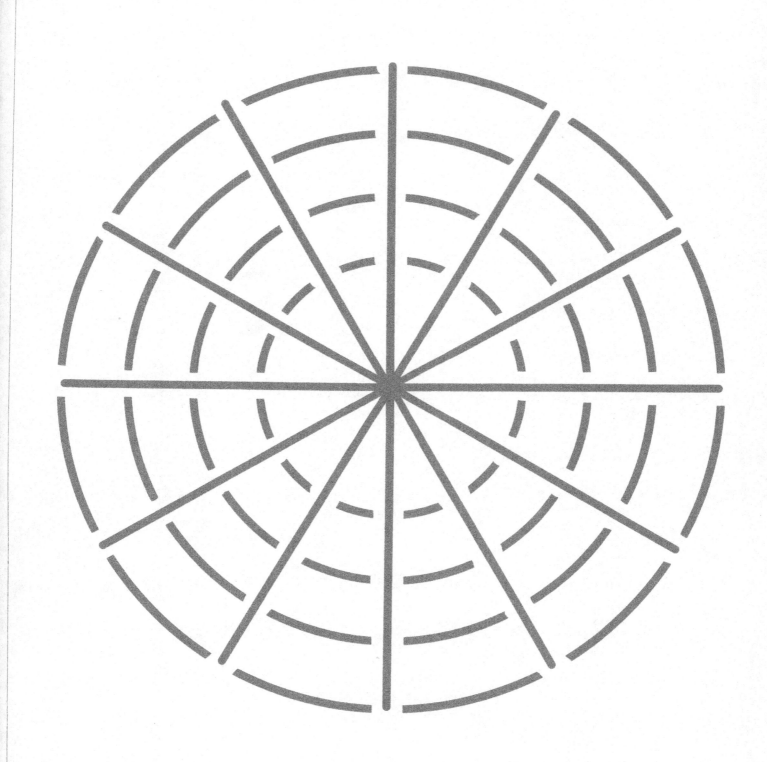

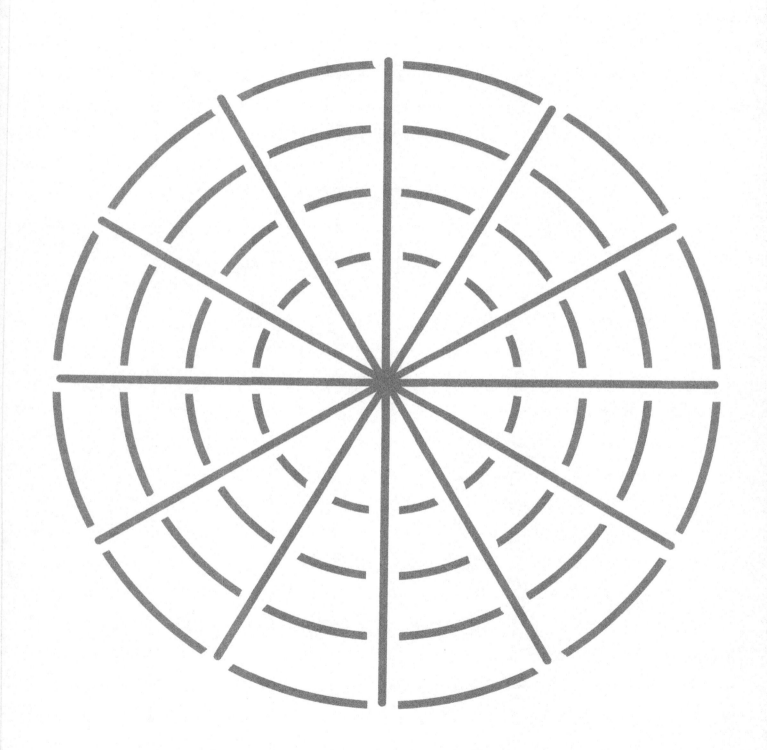

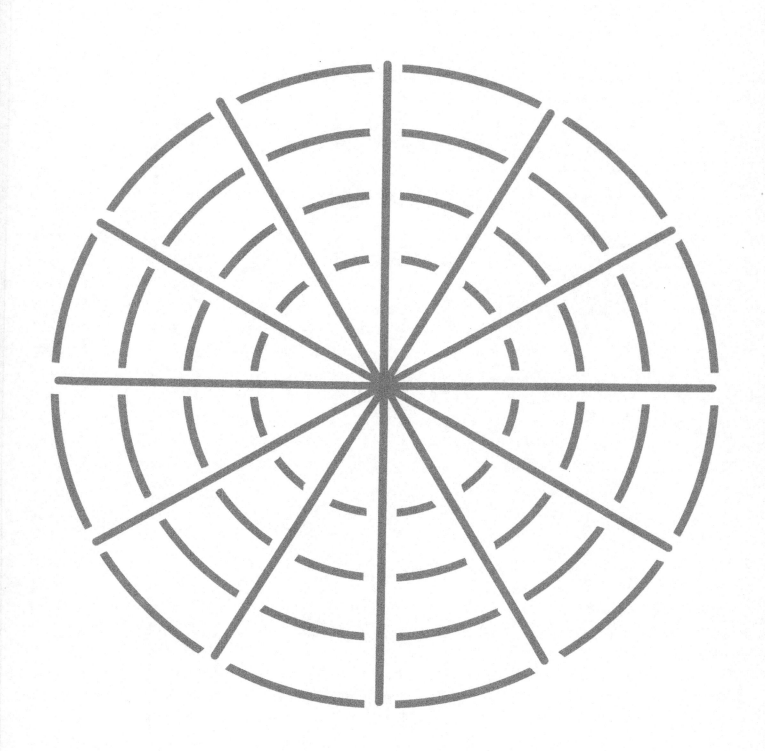

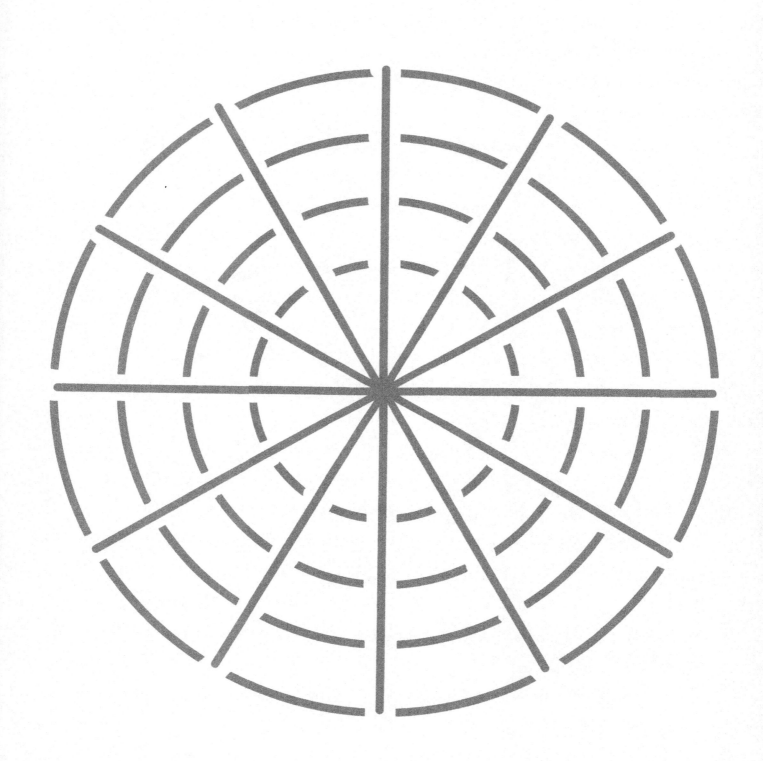

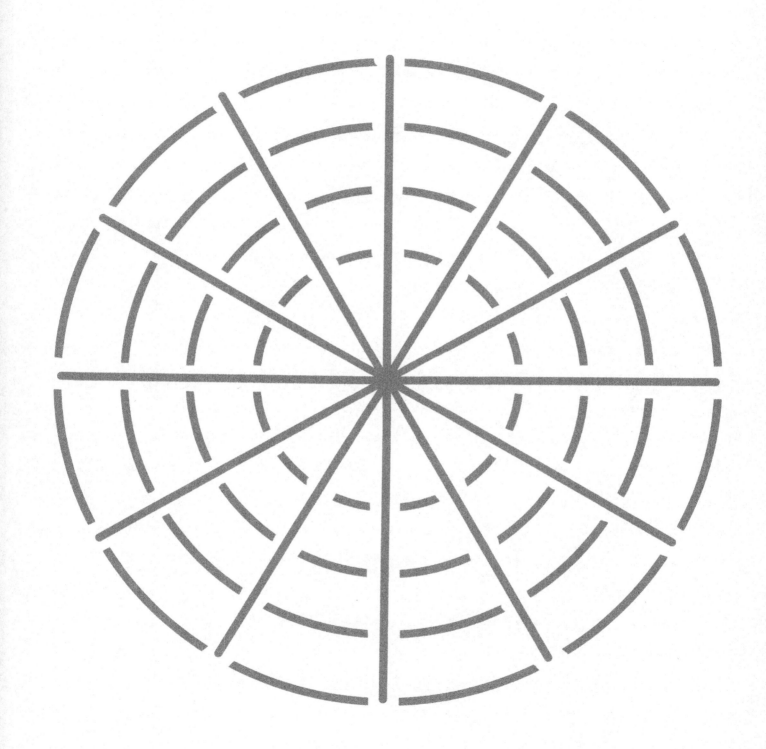

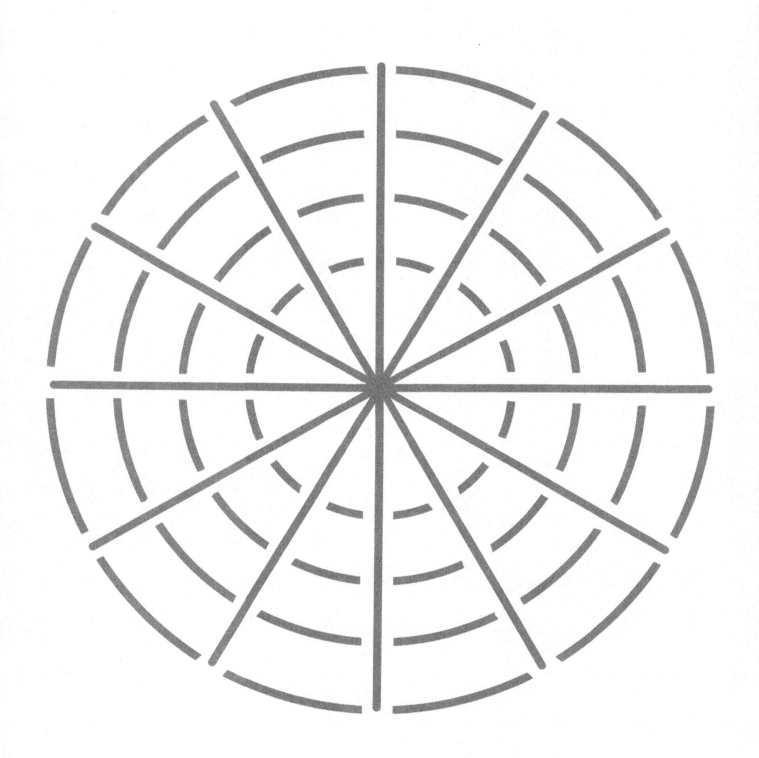

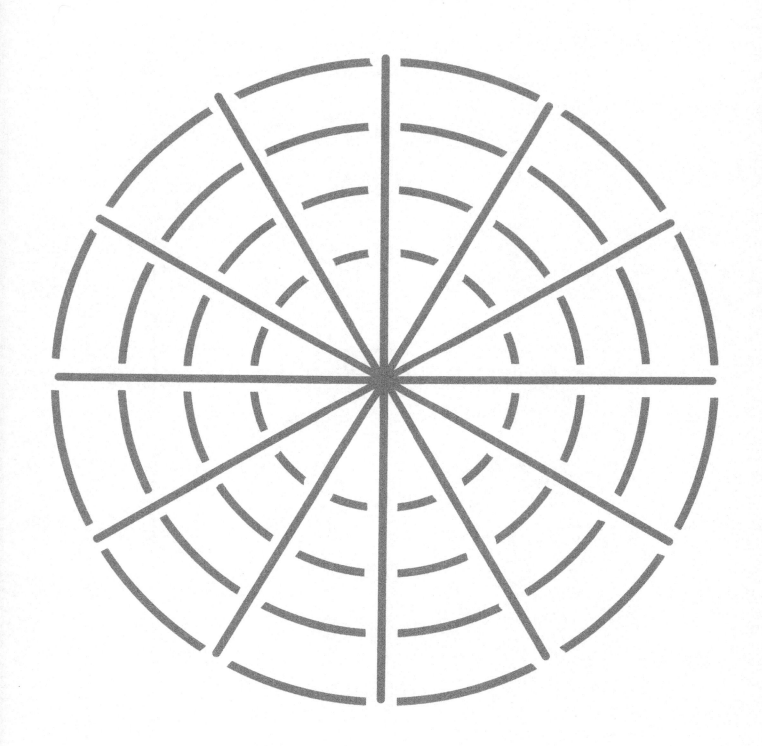

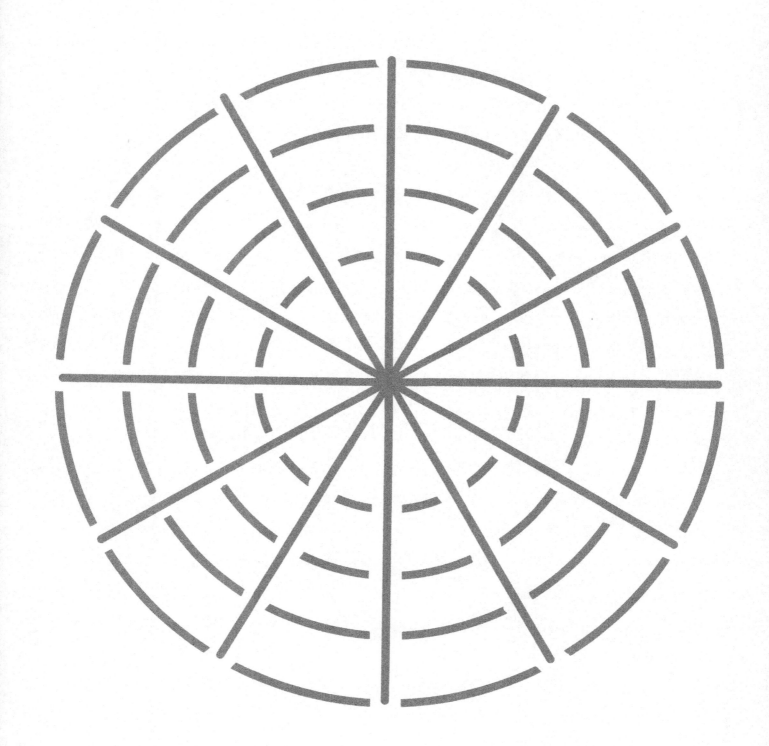

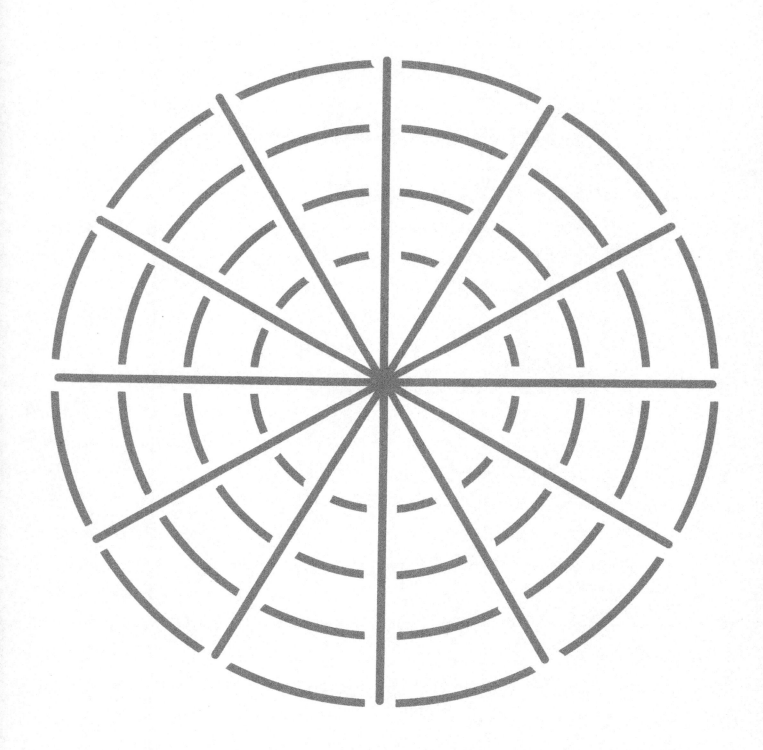

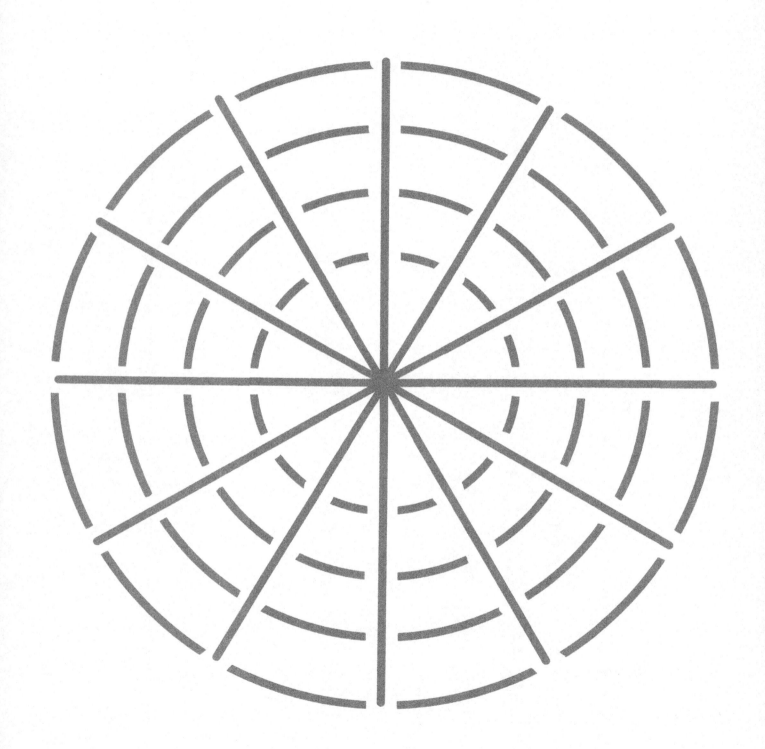

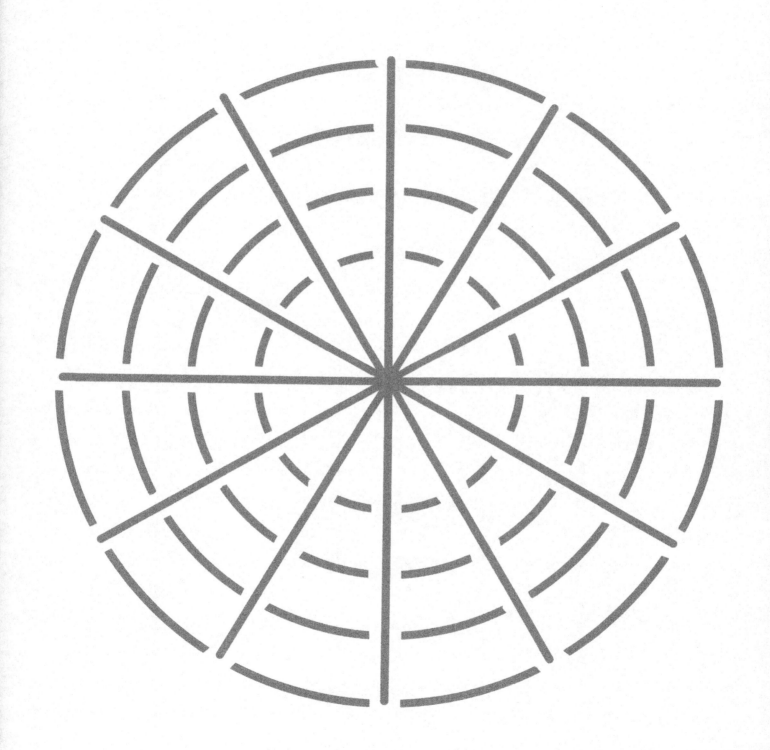

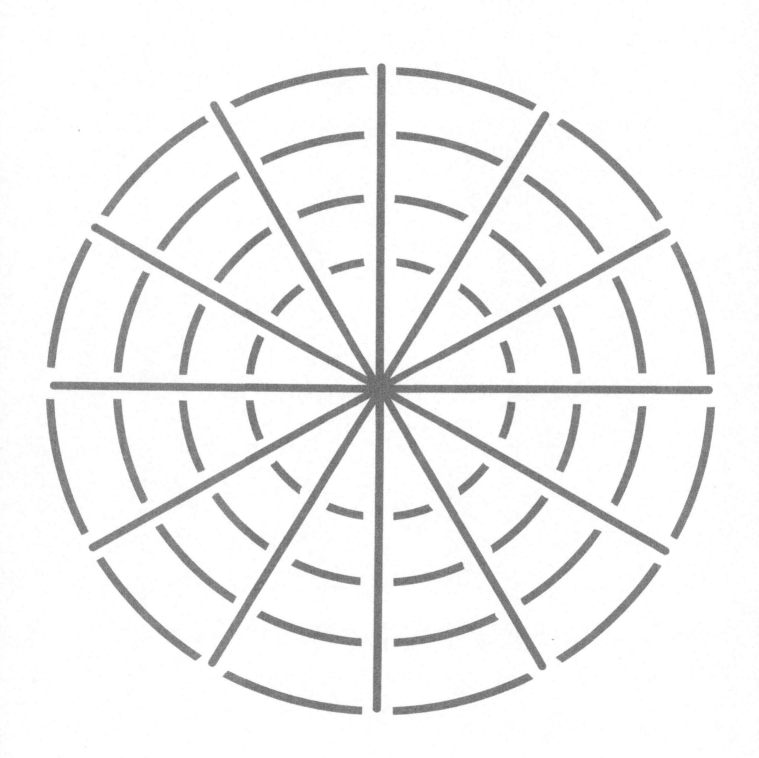

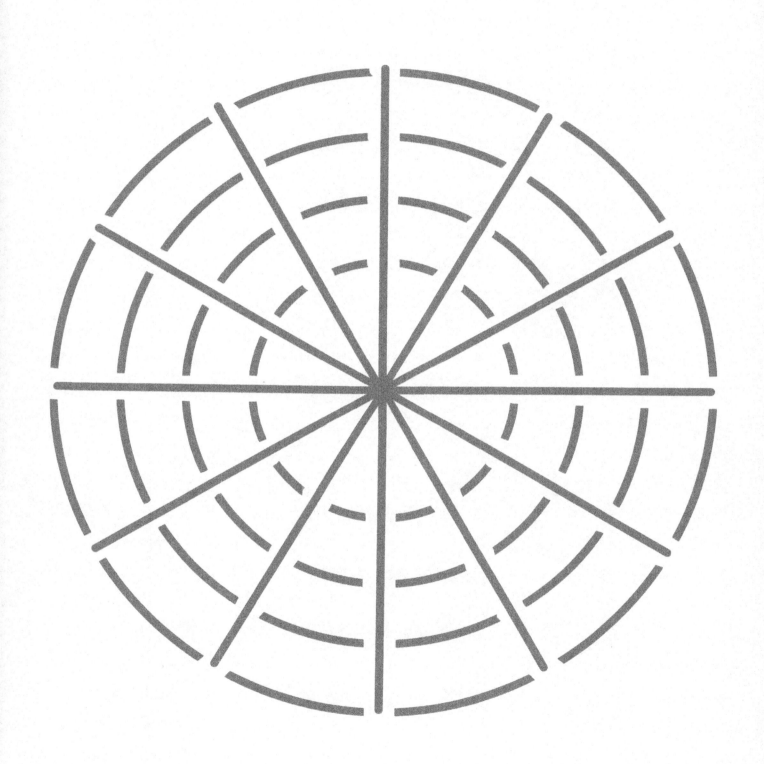

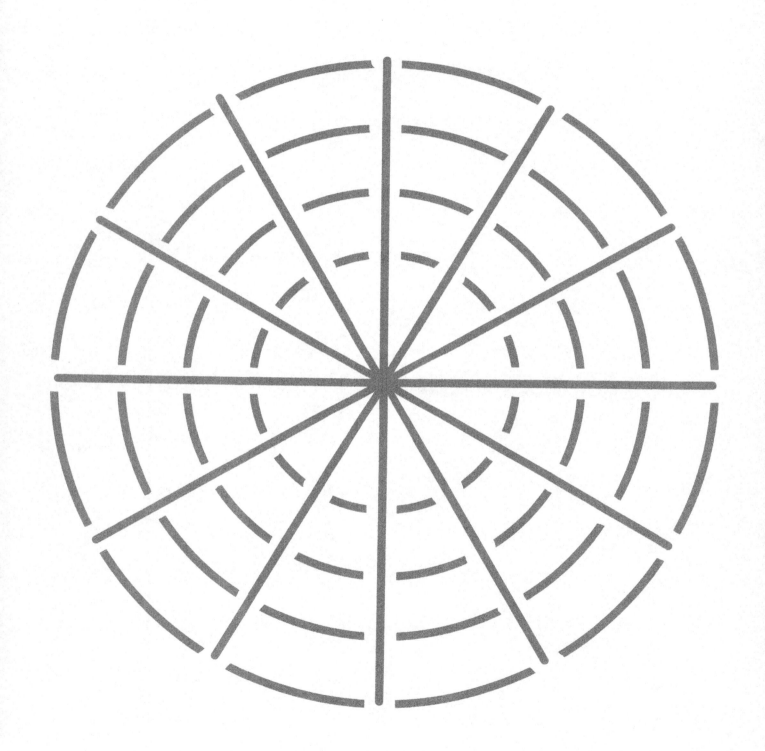

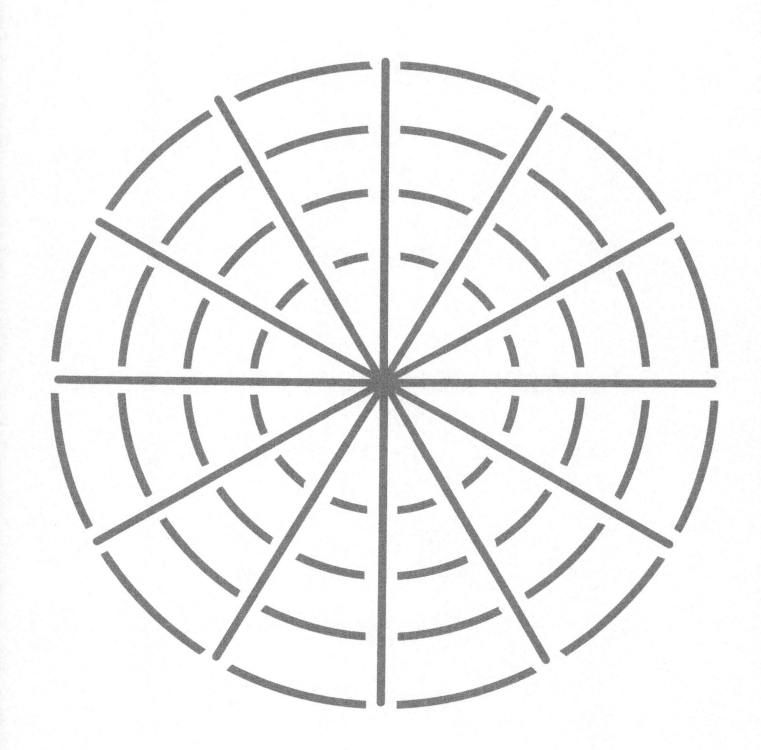

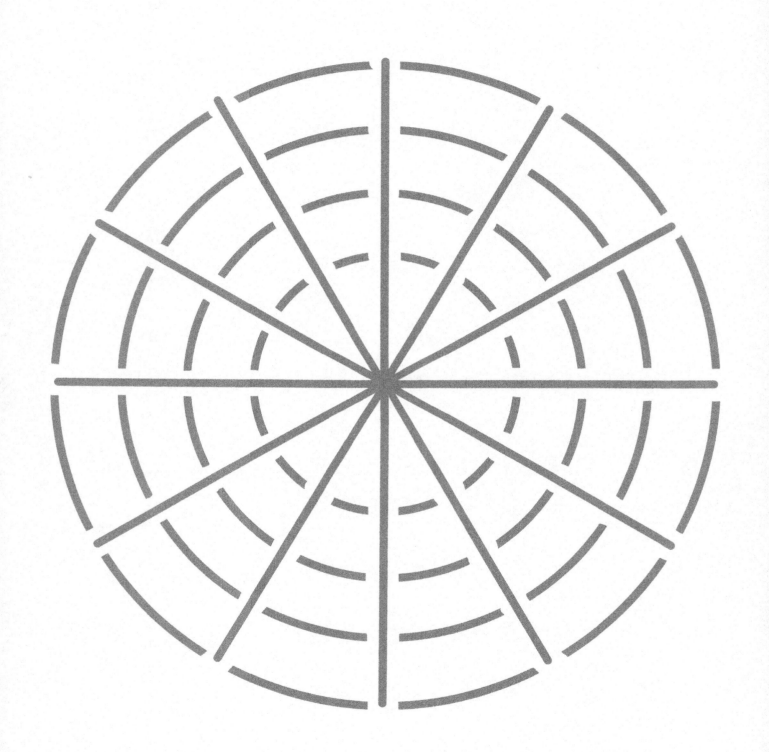

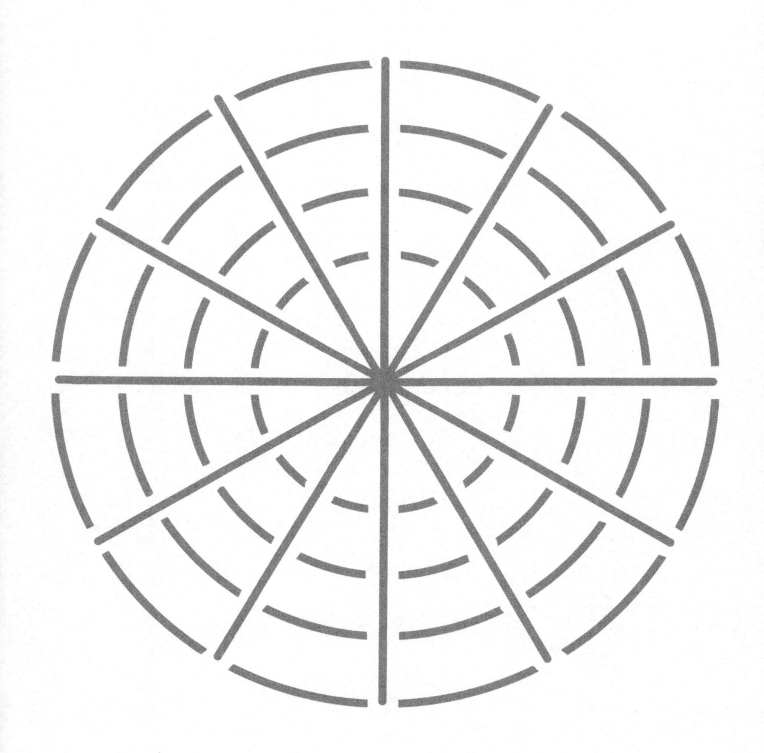

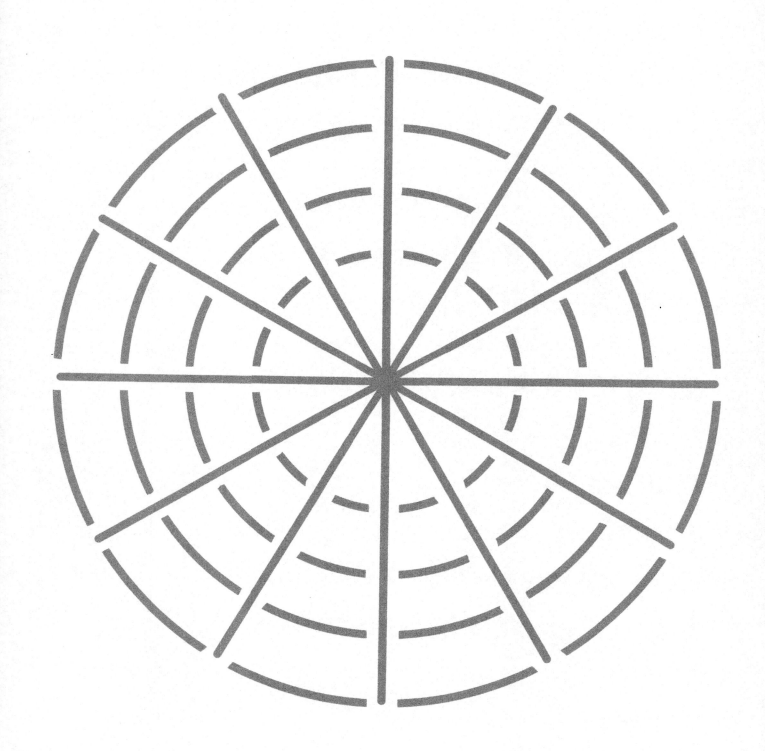

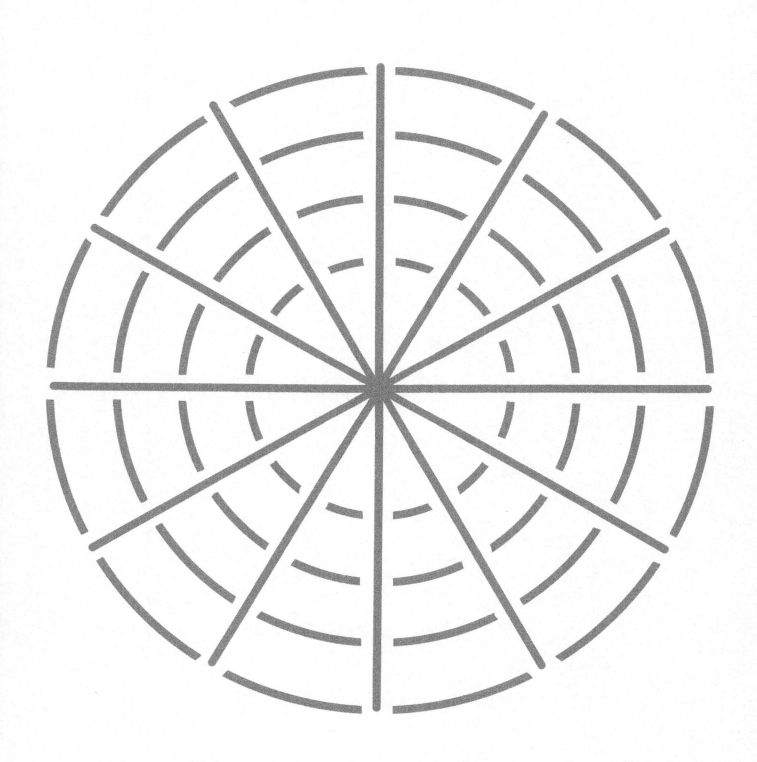

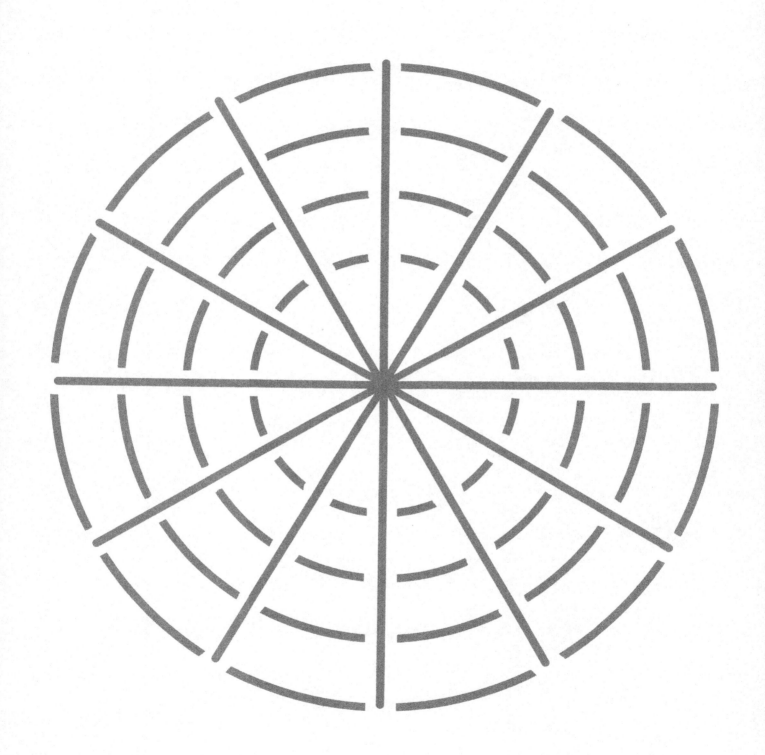

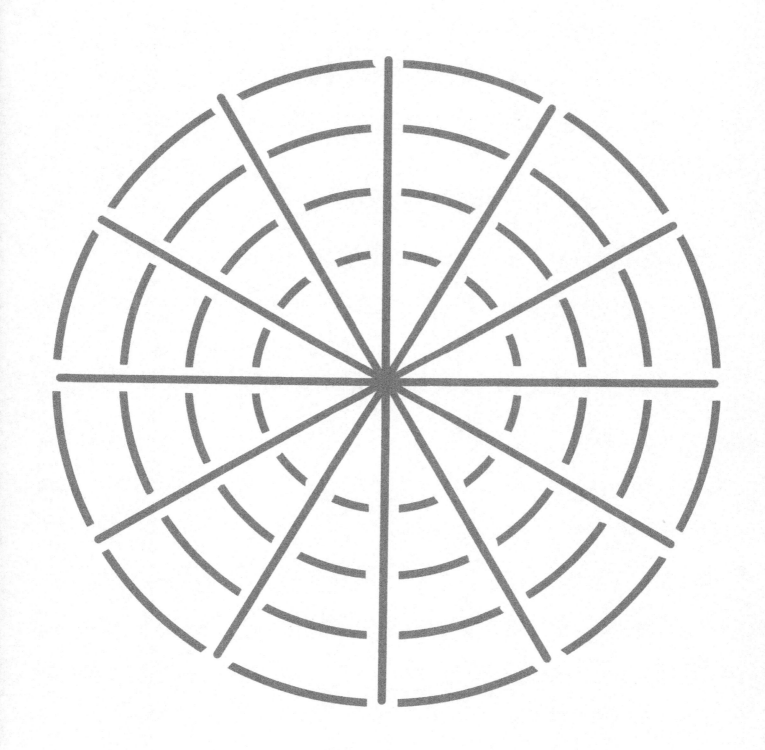

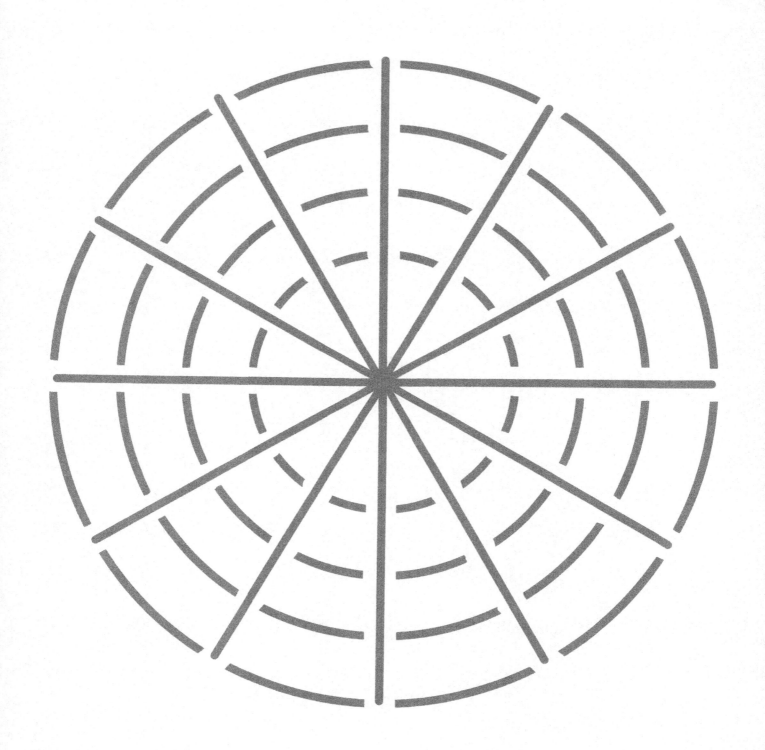

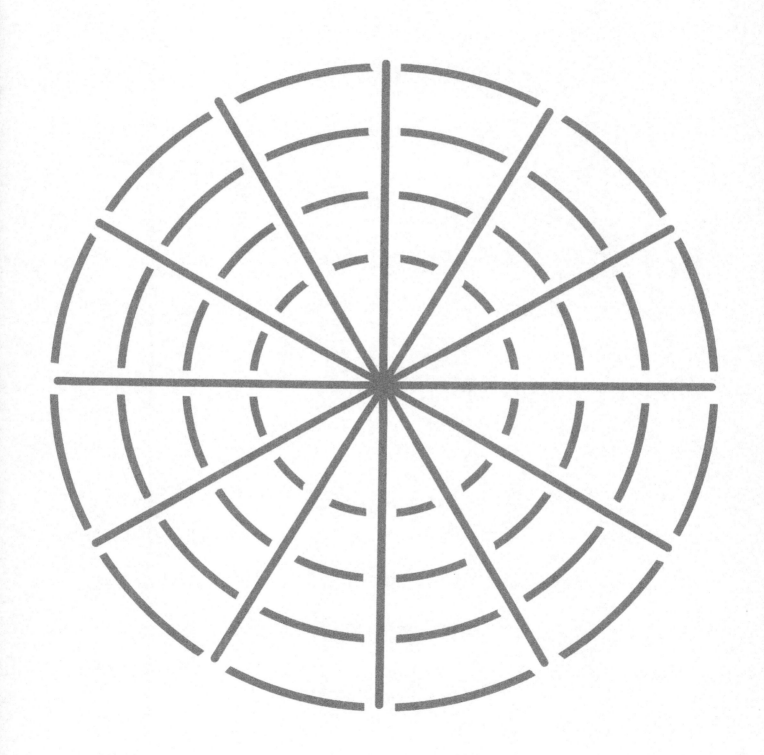

Color the finished dot mandalas according to your ideas.

Printed in Great Britain
by Amazon